BEAUTIFUL ECONOMICS

BEAUTIFUL ECONOMICS

A Guide to Gentle World Domination

How to reboot the world with a new economic narrative

By Howard Collinge

powerHouse Books

BROOKLYN, NY

This book was made from 100% synthetic dolphin skin
and can be repurposed into sexy underwear
or a fat-free, brain-food muffin, but only after reading.

"I'm all lost in the supermarket
I can no longer shop happily
I came in here for that special offer
A guaranteed personality"

THE CLASH

"Lost in the Supermarket"

CONTENTS

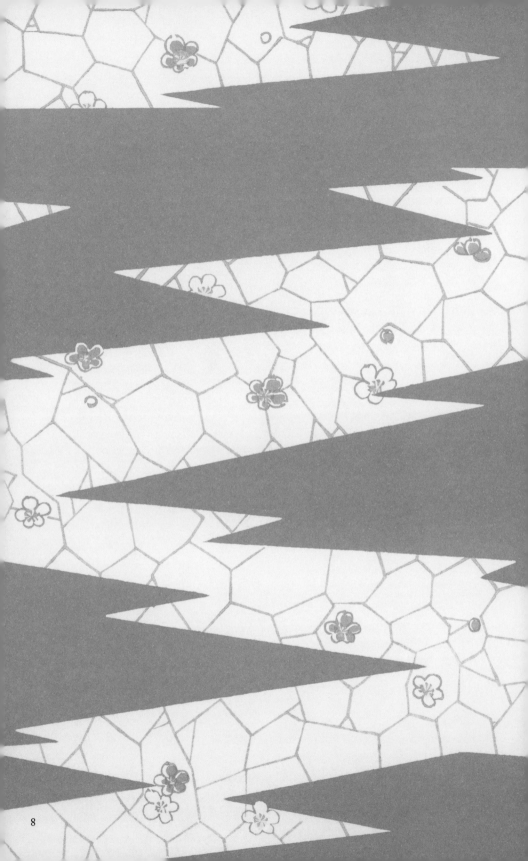

INTRODUCTION

At the time of completing this book, my home of New York City had become the epicenter of the Coronavirus outbreak, and just days from its peak of destruction. Despite also being the epicenter of global economic prosperity, the city could not find enough facemasks or respirators in "the market" to save lives. It was clear that our political leaders had decided to save stock market prices first, humans second. Older people were pretty much disposable in the economic equation.

For the first time in our lives, a virus had exposed our collective vulnerability. It revealed that our economic system is dependent on all of us succeeding, not just the few. If waiters can't pay their rent, then landlords and banks feel the effect. If lowly paid nurses get sick on the job, highly paid Wall Street executives die. We are interdependent, or the whole thing collapses.

On a broader level, the Coronavirus outbreak made it clear that our economic system is highly dependent on our *ecological* system. Nature has its way of reminding us who is the ultimate boss. Whether it's massive fires wiping out regions and species, or a virus that tries to steal our last breath, the economy depends on cooperation with nature for survival, not the other way around.

Yet our economic ideals fail to acknowledge this. Instead, they pit one human against the other, they pit never-ending economic growth against ecological balance.

I believe the key lesson from 2020 is that words like cooperation and symbiosis are no longer just fuzzy-cutesy ideals for the meek, but essential for strength and survival in the 21st century. My hope is that this book will ignite a new generation of activist-storytellers who will help redefine the narrative of economic success. Because to change the world, we first need to change the economic story.

Which is to say, *Beautiful Economics* and its ideas are more relevant than ever.

Here's to regeneration, personal transformation and gentle world domination.

March 25, 2020

1

BEAUTIFUL
ECONOMISTS
WANTED

HELLO, BEAUTIFUL

You might not have a PhD in Economics from Harvard, but you know way more than you think about this all-encompassing, but often poorly explained subject. Economics affects every part of our lives, and it's driven by an invisible narrative that shapes everything we do, including whether you bought, borrowed or stole this book.

Economics is why your sneakers are made in Asia and not Sweden. Economics is why some people live longer than others, and it's why our planet is in bad shape. It's how we choose to live, or are forced to exist, day in, day out. It's also why you're probably juggling three jobs to survive in today's "gig economy." Most of all, economics is an ever-present story that influences what we value in life, shaping everything from career choices to how we treat—or mistreat—other people. If we value and measure the wrong things, we'll do the wrong things.

Which is why economics is way too important to be left to economists. And it's why, to change the world, we first need to change the economic narrative. Money makes the world go round, but stories are what the world is made of.

The world needs a new breed of economist-slash-storyteller, armed with the fundamentals of economics and a million creative ways to tell an impactful and lasting narrative. To influence economic thinking, we need to invent a language that shifts from cold numbers and dollars signs to ideas that spark the imagination and move the body to action.

Don't be fooled by the strange acronyms and complex charts we associate with economics. At its core, economics is about how humans interact and behave with limited resources and unlimited ideas. So, given that economics flows through all parts of life, why not make it more beautiful for more people?

This book sets out to challenge the ideas and language of traditional economics and seed a unified narrative that paves way for a more purpose-driven and ecologically balanced, Beautiful Economics.

EVERYDAY ECONOMISTS WANTED

The new breed of everyday economists will be hyphenated and multi-versed. They might be architects, designers, journalists, scientists or artists. They might have studied economics or worked in a tech company, but they'll also be lifelong students of philosophy and ethics, and perhaps spent time in an ashram, learning meditation. All will have experienced the invigorating energy of the ocean or the calming qualities of a walk in a garden.

One thing they will have in common is that their minds will be adaptable, agile and curious, able to see the interconnection of all things. They'll need to understand the wonders of ecology as much as the prudence of financial spreadsheets. They'll need to let their aesthetic IQ influence their business pragmatism. Most importantly, the new economist's job will require the art of storytelling to inspire the world to live better with less, and profit beyond the measure of money.

Banker–Buddhist Economists

Yogi–Military General Economists

Artist–Climatologist Economists

Hippie–Venture Capitalist Economists

Architect–Farmer Economists

Geriatric–Video Gamer Economists

Poet Laureate–Mixed Martial Artist Economists

Socialist–Billionaire Economists

Silicon Valley–Transgender Economists

Rockstar–Landscape Architect Economists

Fashion Designer–Ecologist Economists

Nobel Prize Winning–Super Model Economists

"We are not going to be able to operate our Spaceship Earth successfully nor for much longer unless we see it as a whole spaceship and our fate as common. It has to be everybody or nobody."

BUCKMINSTER FULLER

Moon · EARTH ⊕ · SUN

SURVIVAL OF THE ADAPTIVE

It's no longer about the survival of the fittest, or even the smartest, because the new economic era will favor the survival of the *adaptive*. Those whose intellect can balance multiple ideas simultaneously, who constantly learn and relearn—plus remain calm and creative while everyone else is losing their marbles—will thrive in the future.

But learning to adapt and transform is not something you will learn at Harvard or any other conventional learning institutions—at least not yet.

In the future, an MBA or Computer Science degree might require immersive field trips into nature to study the interrelation between industry and ecology. The most advanced courses might require attendance at Burning Man to experience new possibilities of social and economic exchange. This cross-disciplinary approach will help tomorrow's leaders see more clearly the connection between London Fashion Week and the microplastics in a child's diet in Indonesia. Or the connection between a breakfast cereal advertisement in Australia and the collapse of bee colonies in California.

The new Harvard Business School of Beautiful Economics will integrate the complex world of creativity, design and aesthetics into business, teaching students to be comfortable with concepts like "beauty" or "informed intuition" or "aesthetic pleasure," qualities that can't be measured on a graph. Every business school graduate and business leader will need to excel in Practical Ethics, so they will develop the acute judgement and vision needed to weigh up the long-term human and environmental impact of all economic decisions.

And for good measure, the most elite schools will require students to go surfing often, because it's fun.

GENTLE WORLD DOMINATION

Beautiful Economics is a more expansive vision of economics where humans and the natural world exist in a symbiotic relationship, giving and taking in effortless flow, in order to survive and thrive beyond the next stock market bubble, beyond the next Fyre Festival, beyond the next generation.

Rather than traditional measures of success like Gross Domestic Product (GDP) which bluntly measures all consumption as positive—we might instead measure the Ecological Flow State (EFS) of a city, which measures the overall vitality of the entire ecosystem, viewing humans and nature as one interrelated loop. In this Ecologic Flow State human and ecological forces ride in tandem, riffing off each other's energy and creativity for perpetual mutual benefit. The human benefits will be experienced as much as consumed, through physical, emotional and sensorial nourishment. The broad economic benefits will "trickle wide" and far because nature itself thrives on diversity and sharing of resources.

Through the union of economy and ecology, and the deeper understanding of the world that results from that understanding, the very best of *human nature* will emerge; the forces of unity and cooperation will dominate over the mindset of acquisition and competition.

The pursuit of "Rational Self-Interest" will give way to the concept of Expansive Self-Interest (ESI), where the individual pursuit of something greater than self, whether in planting inner-city forests or fighting institutional racism, will benefit the self most.

By tapping into our ESI, we will inspire our most ambitious entrepreneurs and businesses to invent new kinds of products and services that serve our higher collective purpose, ushering in a new era of *Green Trillionaires*: individuals who will be so high on life they won't give a damn about private jets, mega-mansions or other stale, pale and male (STM) concepts of power.

*"When lenity and cruelty play
for a kingdom,
the gentler gamester is the
soonest winner."*

WILLIAM SHAKESPEARE

Henry V

TENETS OF BEAUTIFUL ECONOMICS

1.
Humanity is more important than money.

2.
The unit of an economy is each person, not each dollar.

3.
Markets exist to serve our highest common goals and values.

4.
Economy must work in symbiosis with Ecology.

5.
Creativity is our infinitely renewable resource.

6.
Wealth and great ideas Trickle Wide, not down.

7.
Strive to be rich in Life Dollars and
your material wealth will take care of itself.

8.
The success of our species depends on
Gentle World Domination.

MOTHER EARTH, CEO

On a super-macroeconomic level, the planet does not need humans to survive, but humans desperately need the planet. With this simple biological truth, a major correction in traditional economic theory is in order, and we should immediately declare Mother Earth as Founder and Shamanic CEO of the planet. In this new bio-capitalist world, we are merely transient gig workers with temporary visas, each serving our internships on Spaceship Earth.

For the last 300 years, since modern capitalism began to take shape, Mother Earth has been the endless giver in a one-sided and often abusive relationship—giving billions of human inhabitants free rent, magnificent sunsets and endless wonder and enchantment. Today the average person in the developed world has easy access to food (sometimes too much), shelter (sometimes too big) and clothing (too fast and disposable). In return, we've become the planetary equivalent of spoiled brats, making a mess of the oceans and setting our house on fire with global warming—all in the pursuit of free market capitalism.

One day we might look back on this embarrassing epoch of "Ugly Economics," where greed, combined with new-fangled technology and some fanciful storytelling (by politicians and think tanks), justified everything from polluting the air we breathe to profiting from sickness and depression, to giant New York City billboards featuring Justin Bieber selling expensive underwear.

With ecological collapse on our doorstep and an economy that has failed to offer a lasting vision to younger people, much is being said about the "end of capitalism." But this book proposes that we are in fact at the beginning of a more evolved form of capitalism, Beautiful Economics: a vision that simply sees our current, broken system as an immature, egotistical and testosterone-filled pubescent who is a little self-obsessed, impulsive and prone to killing itself trying to take a selfie.

Rather than using outdated terms like "Boom and Bust" to describe the oscillations of the market, we should use the more relevant and urgent terms of "Bloom or Bust," a choice between environmental regeneration or human catastrophe. The ideas of this book aspire to the only sane way forward, through Gentle World Domination.

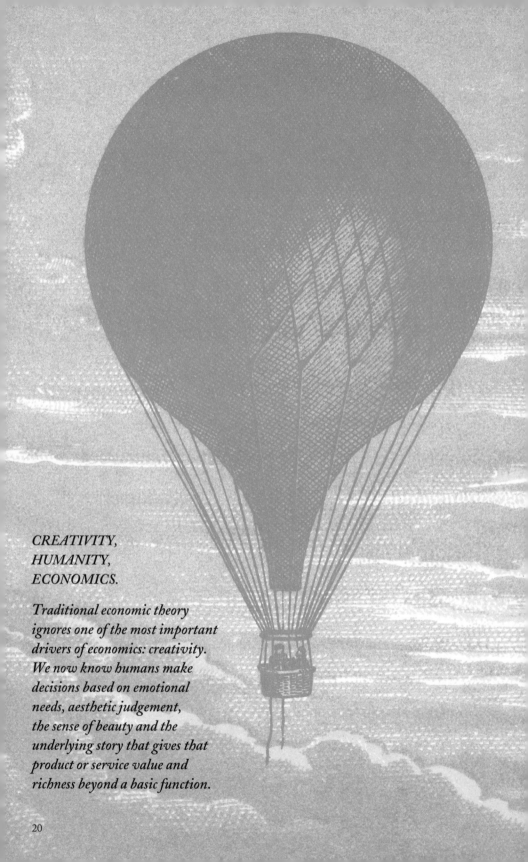

CREATIVITY, HUMANITY, ECONOMICS.

Traditional economic theory ignores one of the most important drivers of economics: creativity. We now know humans make decisions based on emotional needs, aesthetic judgement, the sense of beauty and the underlying story that gives that product or service value and richness beyond a basic function.

THE IDEAS SPECIES

Why is creativity, one of the most important drivers of the economy, rarely talked about in economic textbooks or politics? Perhaps it's because creativity is hard to define and measure, let alone graph.

Creativity is also a function of human behavior, something that traditional economics has tended to avoid. Behavioral Economists are now beginning to acknowledge that economic decisions are not just rational, but more often than not, guided by aesthetic or emotional needs. When a thing is perceived as creative or beautiful, whether it be a shoe, a house or a political idea, real value is added.

We are an "ideas species," constantly changing our behaviors to accommodate new or better ways of thinking. This is evidenced daily by the way consumers are willing to spend more on goods that result in sustaining the environment or helping a coffee farming community thousands of miles away.

People respond to smart ideas, wrapped in stories, even if they pertain to something as complex as the economy. With the advent of modern technology, the transmission of new ideas from one person to another across cultures means that good ideas can make a greater impact on more people, almost instantly. It also means that bad ideas can be weeded out and replaced as quickly as they emerge.

So "beautiful" is not just something reserved for the rarified world of art or fashion, it is an important and necessary part of everyday life. Beautiful appeals to the higher faculties of human consciousness, the part of our brains that can transcend our basic or immediate needs in order to seek greater, long-term value.

BEAUTIFUL ECONOMICS 101

TERMS YOU SHOULD KNOW

Before reading on, here are some important terms and concepts that will help you flow more easily through the following pages. More importantly, they will help you call bullshit on financial media and free market evangelists when communicating economic issues.

RATIONAL SELF-INTEREST

Rational Self-Interest, a fundamental idea behind the free-market capitalism story, suggests that when each of us (individuals and businesses) pursue our own interests, we will benefit each other and the overall economy most. But as you'll see later, this idea is based on a comically irrational assumption, because humans do not act entirely rationally! #irrationalexhuberance

EXPANSIVE SELF-INTEREST (ESI)

Expansive Self-Interest is where the pursuit of *benefit to other*s, benefits the self the most. This is an evolution of the traditional economic concept of Rational Self-Interest (above), which appeals to the lower orders of our reptilian brains. An evolved individual or society must move from Rational Self-Interest to Expansive Self-Interest.

TRICKLE DOWN ECONOMICS

You might hear this a lot in the news media. Trickle Down economics is super-cutesy and noble sounding, but 99% bullshit. It's a phrase used to justify tax breaks and perks for the wealthiest 1% but has little basis in reality.

TRICKLE WIDE ECONOMICS

When they go low, we go wide. Trickle Wide policies generate benefits that radiate outwards, a positive ripple effect whereby more people in an economy spend and invest in goods and services, so the rich can get richer without making the poor poorer. And everyone thrives by helping others thrive.

OPPORTUNITY COST

The opportunity cost of anything of value is what you must give up to get it. Our desires are almost infinite, but our resources are limited, so we have to make choices. But the market economy offers up false choices based purely on "rational" thinking and financials that do not factor in the wider costs (human or environmental) of producing or consuming something.

FYRE'D

When a delusional company or individual resorts to excessive hype, trickery or false storytelling to extract maximum profit from people and the planet.

THE INVISIBLE HAND

The famous Adam Smith (philosopher and economist) phrase has been hijacked by neoliberals to make us believe that no matter what a business does in the name of profit and greed, the "market finds equilibrium." In other words, they believe that the market will automatically "correct" and do what's right and natural. Except when it doesn't, which is often. (see Market Failure)

EXTERNALITIES

The idea that Earth's precious resources are "free" to anyone with a big shovel, or that pollution spilled into oceans is not really anyone's responsibility, allowing governments and corporations to shrug their shoulders with a "not my problem" smirk.

MARKET FAILURE

When the free market crashes or when reckless bankers make huge losses but then get "bailed out" by ordinary taxpayers, so they can pay themselves epic bonuses for their epic failure.

SCARCITY

The problem of scarcity is regarded as the fundamental economic problem arising from the fact that, while resources are finite, society's demand for resources is infinite. Scarcity is a relative rather than an absolute concept.

"No society can surely be flourishing and happy,
of which by far the greater part
of the numbers are poor and miserable."

ADAM SMITH

The Wealth of Nations

ECONOMIC THEORY OF SCARCITY

The new luxury goods: clean water and air

In traditional economic theory, goods that are scarce are called economic goods. Other goods are called "free goods" because it's presumed they are in endless abundance. However, the so-called "free goods," like air and water, are no longer abundant and no longer free. In fact, the reverse is now true and the "new scarce" commodities are clean water, unpolluted air and fertile, unspoiled land.

THE RISING COST OF FREE GOODS IN A DEMENTED ECONOMY

COST

SCARCITY

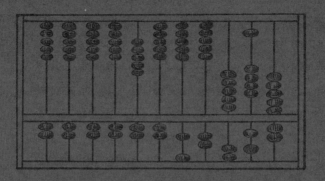

"I discovered
a flaw
in the model. . ."

ALAN GREENSPAN

*Chair of the Federal Reserve of the United States,
1987–2006*

**Alan Greenspan, on the collapse of the financial system in 2008, admitting (to the Senate House Committee) that his
entire worldview regarding trust and self-regulation of markets was wrong.*

BEAUTIFUL ECONOMICS 101

In Beautiful Economics, we are living, breathing, complex human beings with good intentions and bad hair days. Despite being a few DNA strands short of a chimpanzee, we want and desire things that go beyond narrow self-interest and profit-at-all-costs capitalism, because we understand that natural resources are finite and business, society and the environment are inextricably linked.

Beautiful Economics also takes into account one key commodity that traditional economics ignores: Human Creativity. Creativity is rarely discussed in economic theory, yet wherever there is a breakthrough in technology, a better product design or a smart solution to an old problem, creativity is behind it.

In terms of broader economic policy, creative thinking enables us to see the bigger picture and shift our thinking beyond short-term, selfish goals toward the long-term greater good. Beautiful Economics is about creating a new economic model with well-being indicators, true-cost accounting methods that assess natural and social capital and a system of incentives for sustainable production.

Beautiful Economics is also about recalibrating how we value money. We need a new currency that puts a tangible measure on all the things that make our lives worth living, beyond our bank balances. We've called this currency Life Dollars, which we'll discuss further in later chapters.

The great thing is, we all have more Life Dollars than we realize. We just have to do the accounting more often. In fact, if you are reading this, it's quite possible you're richer than Donald Trump or the Queen of England.

HOW DID WE GET HERE?

The version of economics known as "free market capitalism" was designed hundreds of years ago by a huddle of curly-mustached men in suits back when life was, as the Hobbesian dictum goes, "nasty, brutish and short." In those days, we humans were barbarians and things like famine, war and scurvy ruled the world. Today, thanks to the wonders of science and vitamin C, we at least no longer have scurvy.

You'd think that today's version of free market capitalism would have evolved society for the better, but the evidence of barbarism, famine and war is still all around us, perhaps in different guises. This is not surprising, given today's free market mantra which could be summed up as: "Take what you can get, screw everyone else, let our grandchildren deal with the mess."

In our current economic model, humans are one-dimensional units in a giant mathematical equation. If the equation leads to bigger and bigger Gross Domestic Product (GDP), higher share prices and more gas-guzzling car sales, then the economy is doing just fine. This same economic model has produced ever-widening inequalities, with 20% of the world now consuming 86% of its goods, while the poorest 20% consume 1% or less and emit only 2% of the world's greenhouse gases. Something doesn't quite add up.

The so-called "free" market thinking heralds all business as good business, regardless of whether it has come from manufacturing weapons, profiting from sickness or chopping down large forests. The moral measures of good and bad do not matter in free market economics, because economists assure us there's a magical built-in mechanism known as "the invisible hand" of capitalism, which is secretly at work smoothing things out in some sort of cosmic balancing act.

So, when corporate greed is out of control or when our oceans are being polluted beyond repair, that's okay! The "invisible hand" will come to the rescue and do its "self-correcting" abracadabra! So, the theory goes.

So how did we end up with this warped thinking?

The economic thinking that guides us today is rooted in a view of human nature developed into a theory by a brilliant chap named Adam Smith back in 1776. It goes something like this: essentially, human beings are basic, self-seeking animals incapable of making choices that serve the greater good, so we may as well accept this simple human truth and use it to our economic advantage.

This Darwinian view of human nature is certainly not wrong. We are indeed a self-seeking species, each pursuing our own interests, dog-eat-dog, survival of the fittest, etc. But, this is only one part of a more elaborate picture. Even self-seeking individuals know that to ensure their own happiness and long-term progress, there must be strong social cohesion, cooperation, clean water, safe roads, healthy food, education and things that inspire and elevate us beyond the daily dog-eat-dog drudge.

This is why humans need and seek things that are beautiful, whether in the form of human relationships, thought-provoking art, a well-made pair of shoes or simply a beautiful idea, like freedom. Although these beautiful needs are not traditional assets graphed in an economic report, they are no less real or valuable. Indeed, for all this "beautiful" stuff, humans are willing to pay a high price.

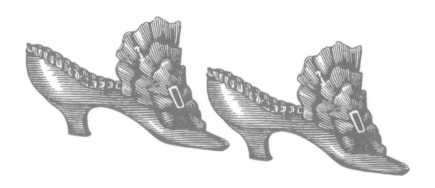

THE INVISIBLE HAND

Adam Smith, often cited as the father of modern capitalism, would be thoroughly annoyed at the way his famous "invisible hand" metaphor, explaining how the free market "self-regulates," has been hijacked to justify greed and selfishness as ends in themselves. Smith's original, and more complex reasoning, is that the harnessing of each individual's self-interest would ultimately lead to a far more ambitious end goal: a more prosperous society.

"By pursuing his own interest he frequently promotes that of the society more effectively than when he really intends to promote it."
ADAM SMITH

Amartya Sen, a Nobel Prize-winning economist, further explains Smith's underlying thinking:

> He (Adam Smith) talked about the importance of these broader values that go beyond profits in *The Wealth of Nations*, but it is in his first book, *The Theory of Moral Sentiments*, which was published exactly a quarter of a millennium ago in 1759, that he extensively investigated the strong need for actions based on values that go well beyond profit seeking. While he wrote that "prudence" was "of all the virtues that which is most useful to the individual," Adam Smith went on to argue that "humanity, justice. . . generosity, and public spirit, are the qualities most useful to others."

What's clear is that the world has radically changed since Mr. Smith's day and that the real hidden force shaping the world is the Invisible Hand of words, narratives and stories.

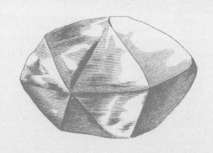

"I'm not a driven businessman,
but a driven artist.
I never think about money.
Beautiful things make money."

LORD ACTON

Creativity is the magic ingredient that can add value to anything from a rubber flip-flop to a city skyscraper. Without creativity, the world would be void of the innovation and life-enhancing qualities of brilliant architecture, laugh-out-loud TV sitcoms, useful iPad apps, stunning dresses, sublime paintings, thought-provoking films and life-saving medical devices.

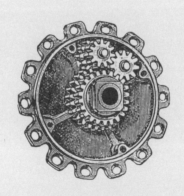

"Ideas shape the course of history."

JOHN MAYNARD KEYNES

BEAUTIFUL GARBAGE

A Beautiful Solution to an Ugly Problem

The problem: New York City garbage piles up fast and litters the physical and mental landscape of millions of people. So why not turn these mountains of trash into another example of New York ingenuity?

Let's turn each mountain of garbage into a colorful art installation, a fun and cheeky solution to a bleak, monotone problem. How? We hand out colorful garbage bags (recyclable, of course) to retailers and businesses. When the colorful, trash-filled bags are deposited onto the street, a mountain of color is made.

Each month, different New York artists could be invited to decorate or design limited-edition bags. We turn the ugly sidewalks into art installations. The city gives a discount incentive to retailers and businesses for using the recyclable colored bags, a small price to pay to brighten the landscape of the world's most diverse city.

1. Over time, our visual landscape can have a negative impact on our psychic landscape.

2. A simple creative idea can turn an everyday eyesore into a playful installation.

THE ORIGINAL INFLUENCERS

THE SHAKESPEARIAN ECONOMIST

Adam Smith (1723–1790). The so-called founding father of modern capitalism published *The Wealth of Nations* in 1776, which despite being radical for the time, went on to become a bestseller. As well as being a rock-star economist and philosopher, Smith was a scholar of Shakespeare. It's no wonder he famously described the workings of the free market as being guided by an "invisible hand," a phrase he possibly borrowed from a scene in Shakespeare's *Macbeth*. In the play, Macbeth talks of the "invisible hand" as a force behind a calculating and bloody murder. Did Mr. Smith foresee what modern capitalism would become?

"Be innocent of the knowledge, dearest chuck,
Till thou applaud the deed. Come, seeling night,
Scarf up the tender eye of pitiful day;
And with thy bloody and invisible hand
Cancel and tear to pieces that great bond
Which keeps me pale!"

MACBETH

THE KARMIC ECONOMIST

Buddha (563 BCE–483 BCE). The original economist, Buddha knew the wisdom of living economically. His economic policies advocated desiring less, not more, using fewer natural resources and more internal resources. He also devised the karmic law of economics, which said something like, "treat people nice, or they return to bite you on ass."

BUCKY FULLER

Buckminster "Bucky" Fuller (1895–1983). A renowned 20th century inventor and creative visionary. Dedicating his life to making the world work for all of humanity, Fuller did not limit himself to one field of knowledge, constantly thinking up new ways to improve life on a global scale. He dreamt up big ideas around improving housing, shelter, transportation, education, energy and the environment. Throughout the course of his life, Fuller held 28 patents, authored 28 books and received 47 honorary degrees. And while his most well-known artifact, the Geodesic Dome, has been produced over 300,000 times worldwide, Fuller's true impact on the world today is his continued influence upon generations of designers, architects, scientists and artists working to create a more sustainable planet.

THE BOOM BOXER

John Maynard Keynes (1883–1946). This polymath Englishman was part of the famed Bloomsbury set, often sipping tea with the likes of Virginia Woolf, Bertrand Russell and E.M. Forster. He saw firsthand the errors of unfettered capitalism when it is allowed to run amuck and create unsettling booms and busts. Keynes devised a way of balancing out the prizes and pitfalls of the capitalist system, so as to protect the vast majority of people from the perils of greed. While "Keynesian" economics is back in vogue, his ideas are still viewed with mistrust. We think it's possibly due to his dodgy mustache.

THE MAVERICK MOGUL

Richard Branson is one of the early Beautiful Economists (B.E.). He has conclusively proven that adding creativity and play to commerce is not only more fun, but infinitely more lucrative. Whether it be music, airlines, space travel or dealing with environmental issues through his foundation, The Carbon War Room, Mr. Branson has always leveraged the exponential power of creativity to transform businesses and people's lives for the better.

CHIEF OF THE BANK OF LIFE DOLLARS

Joseph Stiglitz, a Nobel Prize-winning economist, former chief of The World Bank and former Goldman CEO who advised the White House, Stiglitz has been a bold and tireless advocate of reining in banks. His extensive resume, combined with a penchant for mismatched socks, make him an ideal candidate to run the Bank of Life Dollars.

THE ARTISTIC BUSINESSMAN

Andy Warhol (1928–1987). A graduate of The Art of Business, Andy Warhol wrote his thesis on "Hedge Fund Performance as an Indicator of Art Prices." Having seen the future of investing way back in 1966, Warhol decided the best way to make money was not to become a businessman, but instead to create works of art that businessmen would eventually pay ridiculous amounts of money for.

THE WANDERING CALLIGRAPHER

Steve Jobs (1955–2011). A wandering calligrapher and creative maverick, Jobs somehow ended up making the most beautiful pieces of technology the world has seen. His company, Apple, makes stuff that allows other people to make stuff, an example of which is this book.

ECONOMIC BEAUTY CONTEST

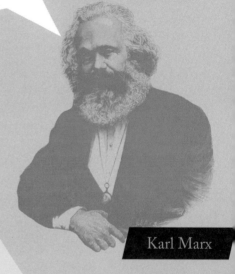

A TIMELINE TO A BETTER TOMORROW

>3500 BC

Homo sapien struggles to exist in nature. Grunts a lot. Often gets eaten on way to supermarket. Discovers flame-grilled bison and invents the "paleo diet" (forgets to trademark).

900—1830

Man dominates nature by cooperating instead of punching. Begins to domesticate animals and develop wheat crops. Feeds his family and has leftovers for neighboring tribes, but charges extra.

1830—2020

Man destroys ecosystems and begins to alter nature's cycles on a global scale. Humans live in crowded cities and factories pollute the planet. Fyre Festival debacle signals The End of Civilization. People begin to complain of gluten intolerance.

2045

Epoch of Gentle World Domination (GWD). Humans work in symbiosis with nature, not against it. People live in urban forests and eat 5-Star cuisine from Vertical Farms. NYC's East River becomes the best place to swim. People still judge each other, but instead by the amount of Life Dollars they have.

WTF GDP?

Gross Domestic Product (GDP) is a measure of all consumption, but it does not distinguish between good or bad consumption or take into consideration the long-term consequences and possible environmental damage. It simply measures all trade as positive, including money spent on military weapons, expanding prison populations, treatment of smoking related lung cancer, quick-fix drugs for mental illness, sales of gas-guzzling SUVs and the chopping down of forests. This worship of growth and GDP has been catastrophically short-sighted from both a human and a business point of view. If we continue to measure the wrong things for short-term gains, we will keep doing the wrong things. It's time we created more comprehensive three-dimensional measures of economic success beyond growth and profit.

SUPPLY
(more creativity)

DEMAND
(more purpose)

Supply and demand and the idea of scarcity are principal concepts in economics. But what we supply and what we demand is entirely up to us.

SHORT-TERM PROFIT V. LONG-TERM DEBT

**Corporate
Profits**

PROFIT

LOSS

Marine Life

War

Landfill

CHANGE THE STORY, CHANGE THE WORLD

Stories Shape the World

Everyday Heroes Wanted

An Economist, a Jedi Knight and Greta Thunberg. . .

A New Economic Narrative

Creativity—A Force for Good

STORIES SHAPE THE WORLD

We think of economics as grounded in science and fact, and we think of stories as separate from reality. The truth is much fuzzier than that.

The economic world we live in is built on what historian Yuval Noah Harari calls, "intersubjective realities": collective fictions created in order for society to function smoothly. There is no scientific or reality-based reason to believe in "free market capitalism," "trickle-down economics" or "US dollars" any more than there is to believe in Father Xmas or hobbits. There are many types of belief systems that are passed onto us via culture or circumstance, but like Father Xmas or hobbits, the stories we believe evolve as we evolve.

Stories are absolutely necessary for survival. We need a good life-guiding narrative to wake up to, whether it be delivered through philosophy, religion, consumerism or Manchester United. If it wasn't for collective fictions there'd be no mass cooperation, the monetary system would break down and there'd be all-in brawls in the Starbucks queue. But over time, some stories just don't make sense anymore. Just as it's no longer appropriate for men to slap a coworker's tush, it's no longer appropriate for man to pour mountains of trash into our oceans. (We knew both were wrong all along.) A new era needs a new way of thinking and, most importantly, a new narrative that hands the keys of planet Earth over to the next generations.

With any successful belief system, whether it be Catholicism or capitalism, the story needs to be told well and regularly, with a narrative of heroes and villains, winners and losers, the occasional sacrifice and a big dangling carrot like Heaven or a shiny Porsche 911.

What will be the big dangling carrot of Beautiful Economics? It may lay somewhere between a solar powered Porsche 911 and the peak of Maslow's Hierarchy, where having met our basic material needs of food, sex and shelter, we seek fulfilment through discovering our individual and collective higher purpose, or self-transcendence.

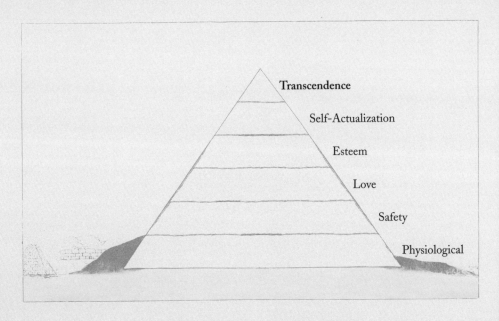

MASLOW'S HIERARCHY

"Written language may have been conceived as a modest way of describing reality, but it gradually became a powerful way to reshape reality."

YUVAL NOAH HARARI

EVERYDAY HEROES WANTED

*"A hero is someone who has given his or her life
to something bigger than oneself."*

JOSEPH CAMPBELL

According to the writings of Joseph Campbell, the renowned academic who studied the world's religions, cultures and myths, the "Hero's Journey" is embedded within all of us. We often don't know what heroic capacity lies within us until we are called to action by the moment in time. When the time calls, it is our highest duty to ourselves, and to each other, to accept the call to action and set out on a personal and collective quest.

The Hero's Journey is a spiritual quest to find our very best selves, with the knowledge that the rest of humanity are at various stages on the same path. The reward of committing to the journey is the elevated feeling of being "all with the world," in which we reach an extraordinary state of flow that transcends all ordinary rewards.

What does this mean for you? It means that your greatest personal journey—which happens to align with the greatest collective need of our time—is about to begin. It might start with a shift in your daily habits; it might start with a well-worded letter to a local politician; or it might start with you becoming a powerful voice of Beautiful Economics.

"There is nothing
in a caterpillar
that tells you it's going
to be a butterfly."

BUCKMINSTER FULLER

Stock Market Boom

Ecological Bust

AN ECONOMIST, A JEDI KNIGHT AND GRETA THUNBERG WALK INTO A BAR. . .

Money might make the world go round, but storytelling is what gives it meaning. Without a great story, facts like climate change or poverty can lose energy. So, what if we took the fossil-fueled ideas of free market capitalism and gave it new energy and a sustainable life?

Like all great stories throughout history, from the Bible to *Romeo & Juliet* to *Star Wars*, there will be a great quest, unseen obstacles and fantastic revelations, a status quo to break out of and a lasting transformation for all.

For the new economic story to impact hearts, minds and spirits, there needs to be a higher purpose that we all strive towards.

So, what exactly is that new story?

A NEW ECONOMIC NARRATIVE

Once Upon a Now, humankind was on the verge of being evicted from its beautiful home. The destructive beast of Ugly Economics had eaten into our lives, screaming incessant advertisements and belching odious gases into our faces. In its trail, it left oceans of plastic, mountains of disposable fast-fashion and a creepy thing called global warming.

For many years we sat around hoping our powerful friends at Davos or our big strong governments might step up, but they were too comfortable with their golden slippers to make any real change. So, we had no choice but to accept *the call to action* and form our own circles of influence.

We began by making small personal sacrifices. We stopped buying stuff we didn't need, abstained from eating cows and withdrew support for businesses that kept feeding the Ugly Economics beast. Occasionally, we attended peaceful rallies and shouted clever slogans.

But that still wasn't enough. Business kept doing their *business as usual*, and so we got overwhelmed, frustrated and threw our hands up in the air, "OK Boomer!" Then, like Luke Skywalker meeting Obi Wan in *Star Wars*, we found a wise guru to light our path. We listened to scientists. We discovered better, simpler ways to live. We saw a better way to grow our food. We got inspired by the millions of brave, ordinary human beings who marched every week. We participated with our thoughts and our actions, and we began to tap into our secret superpower: *Creativity*.

Despite opposition from fossil fuel lobbyists, fake news and corrupt politicians, we used our creative forces to outsmart, out-articulate and out-mobilize the pale, stale and male (PSM) establishment. We used social media cleverly and wrote brilliant letters. We created sustainable new companies. We put our money where our mouth is and divested from Ugly Economics. Our music-lead protest dances were so catchy and mesmerizing, even the PSM joined in! Our ideas trickled wide and became so mainstream that both Fox News and the *New York Times* championed the tenets of Beautiful Economics. We began to speak the language of Gentle World Domination and celebrated our humble Green Trillionaires.

With an inspiring new narrative and a fierce crew of storytelling rebels, we had defeated Ugly Economics and replaced it with something better. Life's balance was restored, and business bloomed spectacularly. Most importantly, we bloomed as a species and transformed for the better.

But unlike most great stories, this one will have no complete or final ending, as the quest of humans to live purposefully and in ecological harmony will be a perpetual negotiation, handed on to each generation henceforth.

CREATIVITY—A FORCE FOR GOOD

Creativity is the most precious commodity of all. It is also the most democratic. It can never be owned by one person, corporation or country. It isn't measured by how much money you have, what school you went to or how pretty you are. It is measured by whether your ideas enlighten or improve or inspire. Creativity transcends race, politics, education and culture. It can spring from anywhere, from the janitor to the science whiz to your mom. Creativity is what makes us human. We are an ideas species. Creativity is our sixth sense. It can lead to sliced bread or a man on the moon. It can lead to peanut butter or Apple computers. It can change your mind, or it can change the world. It can happen in the shower or while eating a donut in bed at 3 am. A good idea costs nothing. Creativity is an infinitely renewable resource. The more we use it, the more we have. Creativity is play, but it is never lazy. It is the hard, gritty, slog of the imagination. Apply it to saving money. Apply it to saving koalas. Apply it to saving the planet. Creativity can make the brain spin with possibility or the belly ache with laughter. It can make cities more beautiful and whole populations happier. Creativity can widen our vision to see the world from multiple perspectives. It is the Jedi force within us all. Use it for good. Let good ideas destroy bad ideas. Creativity knows there's always a better, cleaner, smarter or more generous way. It can lift business and the human spirit. Creativity can make our economy more human, more sustainable, more thoughtful, more useful, more social, more profitable, more lasting and ultimately, more beautiful.

Creativity is a form of superhuman magic that
transforms the ordinary, mundane or merely
functional into something more dynamic,
fun, spirited, sensory, useful and beautiful.
It is the result of a ginormous human imagination
coalescing with dirty, stubborn, real–world
problems in order to give birth to something
mind blowingly distinctive, original and godlike

"You never change things by fighting against the existing reality. To change something, build a new model that makes the old model obsolete."

BUCKMINSTER FULLER

LIFE DOLLARS

The Currency of Life

How to Become a Billionaire in $LD

Keeping up with the Joneses

Life Dollars Rich List

WELCOME

to the

BANK

of

LIFE DOLLARS

A new currency that gives value to all things
that make life rich.

THE CURRENCY OF LIFE

The question of how we value life is central to economics. What we value is what we end up working for. For most of us, life is a daily struggle between balancing our material goals with the pursuit of nonmaterial goals like love, leisure, family, health, spirituality and community.

Fortunately, despite a culture that promotes the endless pursuit of material goals, value is still something we can decide for ourselves. We can ignore the adverts for cars we can't afford; we can stop shopping for clothes we don't need; we can choose career paths that lead to happiness and social good, not just bigger salaries.

Death and taxes may be inevitable, but how we live is negotiable. We can start the negotiation by using a new currency, a type of money that values all the important things in life. That new currency is called Life Dollars, a dollar-for-dollar measure of all the things that make our lives truly rich.

THE EXPONENTIAL THEORY
OF BEAUTIFUL

What do economists know about beautiful?
Do artists give a damn about economic theory?
The word "beautiful" can mean many things,
but in the context of Beautiful Economics,
it refers to something that can lift both the
economy and the human spirit. When beauty
(creativity, innovation, humanity, art) is added
to both business and society, real value is added.

*"There are certain things
that our age needs.
It needs above all, courageous hope
and the impulse to creativeness."*

BERTRAND RUSSELL

Time is money.

Spend it wisely.

HOW TO BECOME A BILLIONAIRE
IN LIFE DOLLARS

The most precious things we have are our health, friends, family, sense of community and time for leisure, play, sport and hanky panky. It's time we had a currency that puts a true value on all these things. Life Dollars measure overall human value and richness. Your Life Dollar value can increase or decrease, depending on your everyday actions. Every time we make an economic decision, we are in fact trading in our own precious Life Dollars. How many Life Dollars did you trade today?

Compare two people:

Person A earns $120,000 in US dollars in her Senior Marketing Manager job but earns only $30,000 in Life Dollars. She has chosen a higher money salary, but forgoing less free time to pursue strong relationships, family, healthy pursuits and community work.

(Real Life Worth = $150,000)

Person B earns $80,000 in US dollars in her Freelance Design job, but an impressive $120,000 in Life Dollars. She has decided to earn less US dollars but is richer in quality of life. With more time available to spend with family, learn new skills, enjoy nature and sunset walks, plus more peace of mind and less stress.

(Real Life Worth = $200,000)

In terms of Real Life Worth, Person B earns less in salary, but comes out $50,000 richer.

KEEPING UP WITH THE JONESES

Even a millionaire can feel inadequate when a billionaire walks into the room. Beyond a certain minimum, all wealth is relative. The "keeping up with the Joneses" mentality pervades all facets of consumer society, whether you're rich or poor. So, here's a simple creative trick. Compare yourself to The New Joneses. Make the comparison using other criteria, like the amount of Life Dollars you have (free time, healthy body and mind, laughter, good friends).

This will not only alleviate your anxiety or doubt about your socio-economic status, but the very act of not caring about your peer's higher salary or fabulous condo will in fact give you more power and Life Dollars.

The psychological shift is subtle, but Life Dollars measure all the important "human-wealth" things like quality relationships, leisure time, love, stress level, community involvement and intense belly laughter.

Improving the overall economy requires both creative ideas and policies that generate both Money Dollars (USD) and Life Dollars (LD), because they are both part of the big economic picture.

THE LIFE DOLLARS RICH LIST

Every year, *Forbes* magazine celebrates the world's richest people by calculating their individual net worth and giving them a ranking, like a football competition. The Beautiful Economics Rich List uses a more three-dimensional approach to calculating wealth, factoring in a set of important criteria that traditional economics fails to measure. By giving human life a real currency like Life Dollars, we are able to make comparisons between earning more money (the USD kind) and earning more Life Dollars. This is not to say that Life Dollars alone will sustain us, they clearly won't. Similarly, the pursuit of money alone will not sustain us either. We all need things that cannot be measured by material assets or bank balances, like beauty. So, whether you're Bill Gates or Joe the Plumber, the more Life Dollars you have, the better off you'll be.

THE LIFE DOLLARS RICH LIST

1.

MR. WATKINS Writer / Meditation teacher / Traveler

2.

PROFESSOR GALLOWAY Podcaster / Businessperson / Boxer

3

MRS. BARKER Fifth grade teacher / Artist / Mother

4

ELON MUSK Inventor / Electric car salesman / Visionary

5.

MARNEY MACRUBIN Vegan chef / Day trader / Roof gardener

6.

BILL & MELINDA Philanthropists / Readers / Nature walkers

7.

COCO COUSTEAU Ocean explorer / Global activist / Expert hugger

8.

MARTHA GREEN Grandmother / Fashionista / Philosopher

9.

BANKS BAUER Skater / Entrepreneur / Poet

10.

WARREN BUFFET Investor / Mentor / Philanthropist

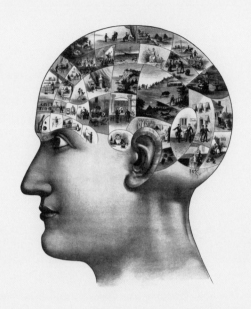

"The more you know, the less you need."

YVES CHOUINARD

Founder, Patagonia

More originality

Less thievery

More leaping

Less tweeting

More jungles

Less concrete

More nudity

Less underwear

More free humans

Less caged chickens

More beauty

Less fakery

More things that last

Fewer things that don't

More community

Less isolation

Fewer nos

Everywhere a yes

STRATEGIES FOR GENTLE WORLD DOMINATION

The Economic Art of Jiu-Jitsu

Letters:

Dear Mr. Cook, Apple Inc.

Dear Mr. Zuckerberg, Facebook Inc.

Dear Satoshi Nakamoto, Bitcoin Mystery

Luxury for the Soul—A Growth Industry

THE ECONOMIC ART OF JIU-JITSU

The Gracie School of Brazilian Jiu-Jitsu will tell you that it's possible to beat a larger opponent with creativity, strategy and patience. One should not attempt to stand toe-to-toe with the beast of Ugly Economics and trade punches, hoping to land a knock-out. Instead, stand back, observe and let its own ideological dead-weight slowly choke itself. Bring your full creative presence and adaptability to the fight and wait for the tiny gaps of opportunity, then strike with purpose.

By staying focused on life's big picture and ignoring the shiny objects of capitalism (consumer culture, status symbols, celebrities), we will reveal its weakness and lack of agility. By leading with generosity and love instead of fear and greed, we will avoid mindless competition and useless stuff. By pursuing lasting community over fast profits and Instagram likes, we will force the Ugly Economics machinery to stop selling our personal data, burning coal or exploiting the poor for cheap labor. This is how Gentle World Domination begins.

Why gentle? Gentle does not mean weakness or lack of ambition. In fact, it takes strength and bravery to show compassion for others. Gentle World Domination is a long-term vision and strategy designed to win the game, while winning in life. It's about staying cool, calm, creative and fierce as hell.

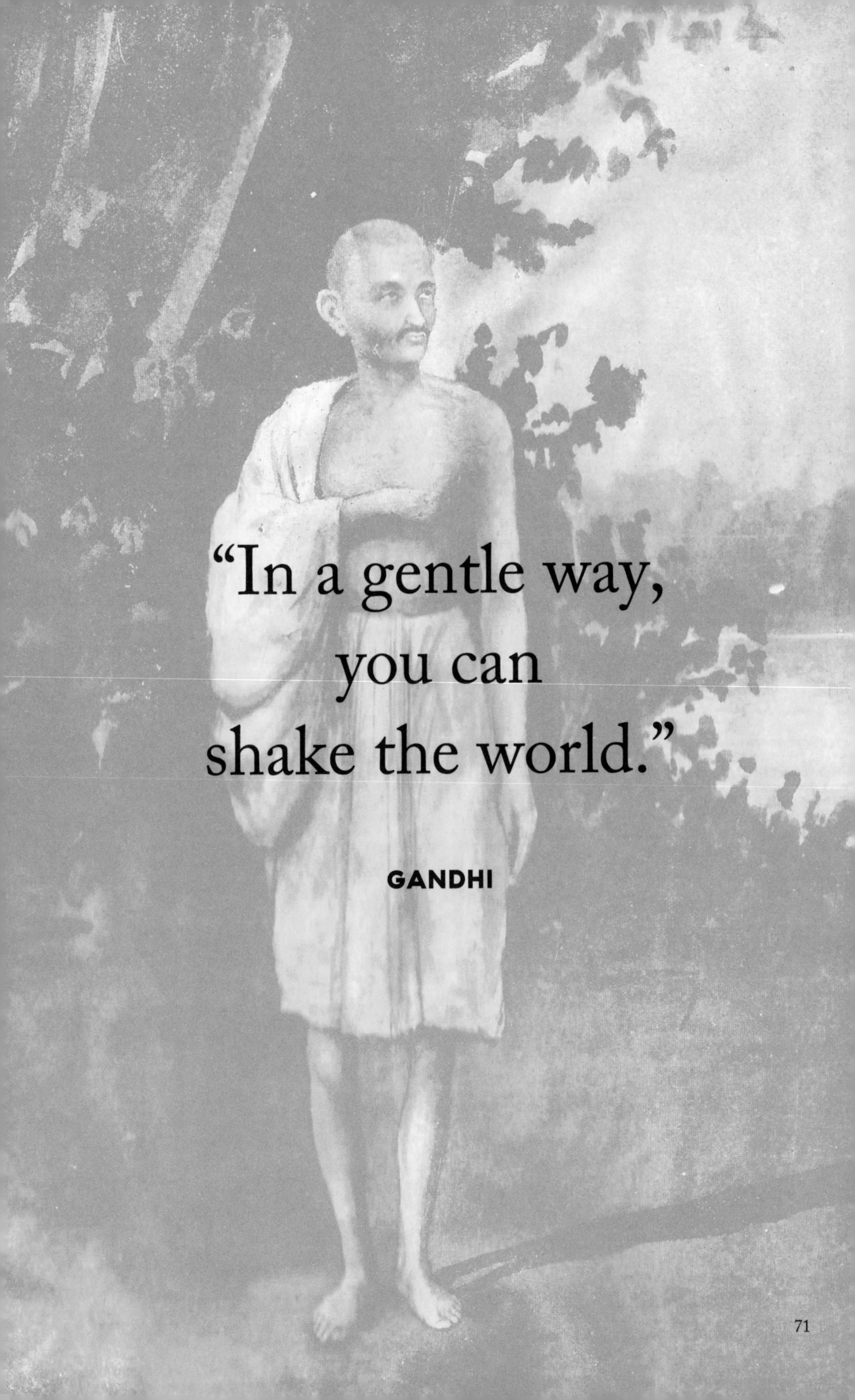

"In a gentle way,
you can
shake the world."

GANDHI

"Being good in business
is the most
fascinating kind of art.
Making money is art
and working is art
and good business
is the best art."

ANDY WARHOL

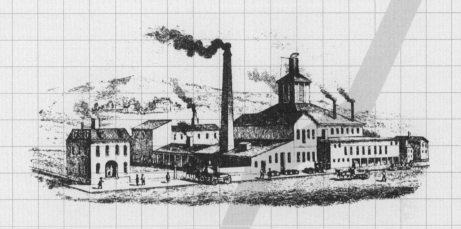

WHEN GDP GOES UP
SO DOES DEPRESSION,
POLLUTION LEVELS
AND GLOBAL WARMING

Tim Cook
Apple Inc.
One Apple Park Way
Cupertino, CA

RE: THE INFINITE GURU, BY APPLE.

Dear Mr. Cook,

The next mind-blowing product by Apple could be something that Steve Jobs would have loved to see in the world: The infinite guru.

Introducing the Apple G, a product that offers just one thing: A wise personal guru. The "G" would learn everything about you, from your wildest dreams to your darkest desires, and help unearth your true talents and your highest purpose.

The Apple G would never share your personal information or try to monetize your life. Instead, it would use your data for good, offering guidance and wisdom for our complex world. Instead of provoking anxiety and self-centeredness, the G would provoke the best qualities in you and nudge you towards acts of compassion and kindness.

It would also serve to help us all make better decisions about the grey areas of life like love, sex and relationships—things they don't teach us at school. Ultimately, it would teach us all to become gurus (teachers) ourselves!

With the Apple G, you could change the world (yet again) by helping us to truly "Think Different."

What do you think Mr. Cook? Green light it, don't fight it!

Yours Urgently,

_____ (Your name here)   __/__/__(date)

Sign this letter and send! Free copy available at beautifuleconomics.com

". . .everything around you that you call 'life'
is made up by people
who were no smarter than you."

STEVE JOBS

> "Every day, I say to myself,
> I don't have much time
> here on Earth,
> how can I make the greatest
> positive impact?"

MARK ZUCKERBERG

June 22, 2017

Mark Zuckerberg
Facebook Inc.
1 Hacker Way,
Menlo Park, CA 94025

RE: THE RE-CIVILIZATION OF CIVILIZATION.

Dear Mr. Zuckerberg,

I love that you dream of making a positive impact on the world Mr. Z., because I have a suggestion for you that combines some of your favorite things: Community, gaming and money!

The idea involves leveraging the power of your social network to bring "non-friends" or opposed groups together to play. Play can change the world, especially when it turns tension into collaboration, isolation into community and virtual world activity into real-world impact.

You'll first need to use your vast data network and stealth algorithms to mine for intersections of commonality between vastly different mindsets and social media bubbles. Imagine bringing together a military general from Ohio with a meditation teacher from Venice Beach to create something useful, beautiful and profitable.

Through the power of video game design, these un-like minds will be challenged and incentivized to solve common problems in a virtual world, each transcending their tribal and political alliances for the common goal. Whether it's combating bullying, fighting homelessness or destroying global warming, you'll see that play pays.

The game would combine the nation-building skills of *Civilization* (perhaps your favorite video game?), social engagement and generous financial and spiritual rewards. We'll tap into each tribe's Expansive Self-Interest—or higher virtues and desires—to create solutions and alignments across political and philosophical fault-lines.

Brands will scramble to advertise with Facebook again as they'll all want to be part of the social good you build. And the more you inspire collaboration and creation, the more you and the players will earn.

Most importantly Mr. Z., your legacy will shine brightly long after your flesh has withered.

Move fast, break things and do good Mr. Zuckerberg.

Yours Sincerely,

_____ (Your name here)   _/_/_(date)

Sign this letter and send! Free copy available at beautifuleconomics.com

Satoshi Nakamoto
(mystery man/woman behind Bitcoin)

Dear Satoshi Nakamoto,

Wherever you are, whoever you are, as the invisible genius behind Bitcoin, I'm writing to ask a rather large favor. It's concerning our rigged economic system, and your mother. Well not your mother specifically, but all mothers the world over. It's an injustice that mothers have never been paid for the thousands of hours of love, care, diaper-changing and gentle guidance they give us. Without the care of women and mothers, who make up half the world, our entire financial system would collapse.

So, I'll cut to the chase: could you please create a cryptocurrency that recognizes the work of mothers and allows them to trade their extraordinary efforts for goods and services, or even paper money aka USD. In fact, every mother should be paid $10,000 Life Dollars immediately, so they can go on a fancy holiday or enjoy a month-long spa in Switzerland.

Of course, this universal life currency of Life Dollars is something everyone on the planet could eventually use. The more we reward people for their valuable, non-material "goods," the faster we change the world, right?

So, what do you think, Satoshi Nakamoto? Are you in?!

Looking forward to *not* meeting you in person.

Yours Sincerely,

_____ (Your name here)   __/__/__(date)

Sign this letter and send! Free copy available at beautifuleconomics.com

LUXURY FOR THE SOUL—A GROWTH INDUSTRY

Stage one capitalism has reached its peak of "stuff making" and will give way to the lucrative business of "experience making," whether it be in the form of a learning experience, laughing experience, adrenaline experience or a psycho-spiritual-sexual experience.

Instead of seeing a giant billboard advert for luscious ice-cream or anti-gravity underwear, we might see an advert for an artistic gymnasium where you'll work-out amongst thought-provoking art and live music to enliven the mind, body and spirit for peak performance and bliss. A great orator or leading sports coach might deliver an inspiring speech as you heave and sweat, motivating you to do things you would never have imagined. Then afterwards, you might slip on the most exquisitely soft, recycled onesie garment that massages your entire body as you sip herbal tea.

Instead of a store selling bath products that promise inner-peace, a new kind of store might offer exquisite head massages and fifteen-minute "philosophical alignment" discussions with an expert.

A new social network might connect us through one of their many green urban spaces (designed to evoke positive spirits) where we can meet others in person, share intimate stories or play cross-cultural ping pong.

Or a car company might design a new vehicle purely around the superior calming quality of the interior, so that every driving experience would decrease the amount of road rage incidents and increase the rate of road love incidents.

STORYTELLING
TO STORYDOING

IDEA PITCH 1 — DREAM DINNER 6

Sustainability that Also Cures Loneliness

What's the problem? In a 2018 report by the U.N., they reported two-thirds of the world's population will live in cities by 2050. In many cities, people live alone and will rely heavily on food delivery services. That's a lot of lonely people, and a lot of plastic take-out containers.

The Solution: Dream Dinner 6
A sustainable food delivery service that brings you reusable or biodegradable packaging, plus six virtual dinner guests of your dreams. The guests will be leading figures from all cultures and history, so you can share your pizza with Cleopatra, Bono, Barack Obama and Princess Leia at the press of a button.

With each subscription to Dream Dinner 6 we'll include a VR set from which you can select your emotional mood, dinner setting and the guest list. You can curate your guest list according to your emotional needs at the time, whether you're feeling sad, flat, happy or in need of some uplifting advice.

Tonight's menu will be Korean BBQ, set in an open field in France. Now choose six dinner guests:

David Bowie	Cleopatra
Muhammed Ali	**Lara Croft**
Scheherazade	Keith Richards
Michelle Obama	**Adam & Eve**
Rimbaud	James Baldwin
Stormy Daniels	**Brian Eno**
Hunter S. Thompson	Yanis Varoufakis
Ada Lovelace	**Gil Scott-Heron**
Bill Murray	Coco Chanel
Mariana Mazzucato	**Ali Wong**
Keanu Reeves	Zadie Smith

IDEA PITCH 2 — GRANDMOTHER EARTH

Saving Grandmothers while Saving Fashion

What's the problem? For the first time in history, people aged 65 and over will soon outnumber children under the age of 5. Elderly women and grandmothers, who make up over half of the projected 83.7 million* older citizens, are the most undervalued and underutilized assets in our society. The world's aging population will soon create a class of forgotten people who will need social engagement as well as income.

The other old problem: the fashion industry is one of largest polluters in the world.

The Solution: GRAMZ

A 100% recycled luxury fashion brand, crafted and assembled by the loving hands of "grandmothers" and designed by young talent. This will be an intergenerational and intercultural collaboration that gives back to our "grandmothers," while recycling luxury goods and clothing. This business model shifts the manufacturing away from cheap labor towards well-paying jobs for the women who created all of us—our grandmothers.

How:

Take your old, damaged or ill-fitting clothing to your local "Gramz Corner," which partners with every laundry on the planet, and we'll restore, re-purpose and regenerate your clothing to your new needs. It will take up to 4-6 weeks, but with the hand-made grandmother love and attention, combined with clever hipster upgrades from young designers, your new Gramz item will be more valuable and lasting than it was before. And you will have helped sustain a community of local grandmas, maybe even your own.

In 2050, the population aged 65 and over is projected to be 83.7 million
2012 National Projections. United States Census Bureau

IDEA PITCH 3 — REWILDING RETAIL

Wild Retail Experiences

What's the problem? American malls are dying. Retail store closures are sweeping the country. According to a report by Credit Suisse in 2017, between 20% to 25% of malls will close by 2022.

The solution: Turn the thousands of abandoned retail malls into Wild Retail Experiences, a place for ecological learning, music and full-cycle retail experiences. At this "green mall" customers will be able to see, hear, feel and learn how food and products are made, and be part of the entire process from beginning to end. It will combine vertical farming technology with experiential learning, allowing people to reconnect with nature's cycles.

Wild Retail Experiences (WRE) responds to a growing need for experiential travel and life-long learning, in a social setting. People will be able to shop for whole foods and enjoy rooftop farm-to-table meals, as well as get their old clothes recycled and redesigned on the spot. Wild Retail Experiences would partner with leading sustainable brands as well as conservation foundations, eco-experts and learning institutions.

*"Growth must end.
Our economist friends don't
seem to realise that."*

VACLAV SMIL

Environmental Scientist

THE BANK OF LIFE DOLLARS—SAVING TIPS

1. INVEST IN AIR

Invest your time in things that inspire you or make your Life Dollars account grow. Invest in turning good relationships into great relationships. Invest at least 10 minutes a day to smell the roses or watch a sunset, and simply marvel at the fact that a meteor hasn't crashed into the Earth and made you extinct. All these activities pay dividends in ways that can't be counted on a bank statement.

2. DON'T SAVE

Saving Life Dollars is for suckers. Keep the currency flowing; the more you give away, the more you earn. Don't wait for the next person or the next job or the next life. Don't save your creative talent for a retirement that might never arrive. Life is happening right now and the more we try to save, the more we spill. So don't save or be too safe, just spend, spend, spend your Life Dollars and spend wisely.

3. SPECULATE

Dream, imagine, think big and be prepared to be called a lunatic, at least until people understand your true genius. Do something that will make your one-and-only short life extraordinary. Do something that matters to you, not your brother-in-law's neighbor. Don't settle for what your parents or your expensive education or those glossy magazine adverts told you was best for you. When you think creatively, everything is malleable. The more we speculate a healthier, happier, richer way to live, the more we can make it happen.

4. HEDGE

Bet against a world that behaves as if natural resources are infinite. Go against the economic thinking that tells you growth is the only way forward. Take a position when politicians tell you the best way to stimulate the economy is to buy more stuff. If a hedge fund banker is buying a Warhol for $2 million, don't become a hedge fund banker, become the next Warhol. Not joining the herd will set you apart, making you a more valued, and valuable commodity.

5. AVOID TAX

You cannot avoid death, but the IRS can never tax your Life Dollars!

6. GAMBLE

Creativity is about throwing some mental dice on the table and seeing where they land. Creativity takes on the odds and is prepared to lose. It takes courage to pursue a creative life, but the Life Dollars payout can be spectacular. So, step into those garish flashing lights and gamble your genius until you get tossed onto the street by security. Who cares if you occasionally lose, right?

7. GIVE IT AWAY

You may not have as much cash as Bill Gates, but you can be a generous Life Dollars philanthropist! In fact, the more Life Dollars you give away, the more you earn. The Karmic Laws of Economics apply here, for simply spreading Life Dollars around means that you're encouraging more people to give away too, which ultimately means Life Dollars will circulate back to you.

8. LIVE OFF THE INTEREST

Most super-rich folks simply live off the interest of their investments. You can too! The more Life Dollars you have in the bank, the more radiant energy and confidence you will exude. People will sense you have something desirable. Small children, puppy dogs and super models will gravitate to you. Grumpy old men will smile at you. Religious sages will seek your company. Good things will generally come your way.

THE DIVESTMENT FIRM

There's power in voting with your Life Dollars (e.g. your time, attention, passion). If overnight, thousands of people withdrew their attention and/or financial support from a company who supported disinformation, sexism, racism or Ugly Economics of any kind, that company would get seriously nervous and begin to rethink its profit-at-all-costs behavior.

Divestment, or pulling your support from companies or brands that are not acting for the long-term benefit of humankind, is a powerful way to make large structural changes if the numbers are large enough.

The ripple of change can start with one person. Start with the facts, then get creative. Develop a mini-campaign, amplify the truth and explain how the collective effect of millions of people shifting their attention to businesses that do the right thing can transform the market.

If this seems drastic or overly ambitious, simply start by divesting your own attention from time-wasting apps or ephemeral retail comforts, and the ripple effect will begin to radiate out to those around you.

"Nature is trying very hard
to make us succeed,
but nature
does not depend on us.
We are not the
only experiment."

BUCKMINSTER FULLER

THE ROAD TO SURFDOM

Kelly Slater in a mash-up with dead Austrian economist, Friedrich Hayek

1.

1769 Tahiti. Naturalist Joseph Banks reports seeing a local Chief riding waves gracefully on planks of wood. Mr. Banks was reportedly "stoked" on seeing this and made a primal, "Woooohoo!!" cry.

2.

1966 California. A group of rebel drop-outs decide that surfing is infinitely more rewarding than sitting in an office all day shuffling paper. They were right.

3.

1969 Australia. During the cold winters of Bells Beach, a group of inventive surfers experiment with crude rubber outfits called "wetsuits." A little company called Rip Curl is born, giving birth to a multibillion-dollar surf and lifestyle company.

4.

1970 Young men "surf" the pavement on miniature surfboards mounted with innovative polyurethane wheels. Government and sensible folk frown at these skateboarding hoodlums. The skateboarding industry booms.

5.

1970s A former Rip Curl employee forms a competitor brand, Quicksilver. The competition leads to innovation of lighter and stronger materials, aerodynamic fins and precision, radical hairstyles.

6.

1980s Everyone from hedge fund bankers to soccer moms take up surfing. Surfers must look cool, so they spend money on stuff like zinc cream and boardshorts and sunglasses. The ripple effect of economics.

7.

2030 Surfers ride "iceberg" waves in the South Pole with paper-thin wetsuit material made from synthetic dolphin skin. Scientists and oceanographers begin using terms like "totally sick!" and "getting air" in academic research papers.

8.

2037 Shark Repellent Spray launches (finally).

9.

2040 Interspecies iPhone app. A new app that allows humans to talk directly with other species. Sharks turn out to be quite reasonable characters and a peace truce is made. (Shark Repellant Co. goes out of business.)

10.

2054 Sky surfing launches, a combination of flying and surfing using wind-energy "jet-propulsion." Sky surfing becomes the preferred mode of transport, spawning yet another fun-driven industry.

Creativity brings,

LIGHT *to* TRUTH

MOTION *to* FACTS

ACTION *to* VISION

ENERGY *to* FATIGUE

REALITY *to* IDEAS

DESIGN *to* DISORDER

"Man sacrifices his health in order to make money. Then he sacrifices money to recuperate his health.

And then he is so anxious about the future that he does not enjoy the present; the result being that he does not live in the present or the future; he lives as if he is never going to die, and then dies having never really lived."

THE DALAI LAMA

7

THE NEW METRICS

Love & Economics

Art & Economics

Play & Economics

Freedom & Economics

Peace & Economics

Life & Economics

LOVE & ECONOMICS

In economics, there are two kinds of love. There is the fleeting, one-night-stand kind of love (short-term profits) and there's the true and lasting kind of love (long-term profits, with dividends). In economic terms, we are not only in an age of quick-fix love, but we're stuck with an unhealthy addiction to fake-tanned call girls who overcharge and underperform.

On a personal level, we juggle daily our pursuit of love with the pursuit of career and money. Love and economics have long been unspoken bedfellows, from the economically viable Mr. Darcy in Jane Austen's *Pride and Prejudice*, to the "supply and demand" story of the prostitute and banker in the hit movie, *Pretty Woman*. Love rules, and economics is often part of the equation.

Like love, economics is a constant dance between what the head thinks and what the heart desires. Traditional economic theory presumes that human beings make rational choices, leading to predictable and measurable outcomes. The truth is that our relationship with economics is one of crazy mood swings and temper tantrums. Alan Greenspan, the former US Federal Reserve Chairman and mood-swinger, coined the phrase "irrational exuberance" to describe investors during the 90s dot-com boom.

In Wall Street-speak, the word "sentiment" (i.e. feelings) is often used to describe the market. The market can be either "bullish," where people are feeling confident (over-confident) and sometimes greedy, or "bearish," when an overriding feeling of fear and insecurity rules. If we continue to allow these extreme animal spirits of the bull and the bear to guide our relationships (financial or otherwise), we're doomed to rocky short-term relationships and messy break-ups.

Instead of worshipping bulls and fearing bears, perhaps it's time we introduced a new animal spirit to inspire us toward wiser economic choices. Perhaps it's time we introduced the unicorn.

"With $10,000 we'd be millionaires!
We could buy all kinds
of useful things like…love!"

HOMER SIMPSON

"When bankers get together,
they talk about art.
When artists get together,
they talk about money."

OSCAR WILDE

ART & ECONOMICS

Since the powerful Medici family of 15th century Italy, art has been associated with money and banking. But never before has there been so much money thrown at so much art. In 2011, the art market outperformed the S&P 500 index of US equities by about 9 percentage points—largely driven by increased Chinese demand and high prices for the work of popular artists such as Andy Warhol.

One of the genius business deals of the century came when Damien Hirst, an artist, sold his entire art collection for a staggering $200 million, just hours before Lehman Brothers imploded. Did Mr. Hirst know something that Wall Street bankers didn't?

Where would art be without bankers? Where would bankers be without art? Art has imitated economic life in that it has enlisted the techniques of marketing and PR to increase an artist's "brand" value. The most financially successful artists today are often marketed like brands, much like Mr. Warhol's Campbell's soup cans.

But does that make them more valuable artists? Of course, art and artists have a far greater value outside of the increasingly small world of the art market. Perhaps the most important role of art and creativity is to redefine the way society sees and values things, beyond the measure of material wealth. Art and artists are a fundamental part of turning Ugly Economics into Beautiful Economics.

PLAY & ECONOMICS

Play, an activity seemingly reserved for children, dolphins and Hugh Hefner, is not the frivolous pastime we're taught to believe. In fact, play is a seriously important process that can lead to grand outcomes. Without play, there is no risk; without risk, there is no innovation.

"A man's maturity is to have rediscovered
the seriousness he possessed as a child at play."

FRIEDRICH NIETZSCHE

Play is a serious business. In monetary terms, play, and its biproducts laughter and well-being, are highly sought-after commodities, generating billions for the makers of entertainment, toys, video games and outdoor playgrounds. Both children and adults benefit from play—physically, mentally and emotionally. When play is added to education or the workplace it increases learning, relieves stress and makes us more productive.

But somewhere between childhood and adulthood, we lose the sense of play. We exchange play for work and responsibility, as if they are incompatible. But our most successful and innovative companies know that play leads to pleasure and happiness, which leads to better long-term productivity. So, it turns out that what is good for the human spirit is also good for business.

So, let's demand that play be part of our private and public spaces, our workplaces and our educational institutions. Ask your boss for a "Playrise" as well as a pay rise. Organize regular "play dates" with your partner. Don't just play to win, play to live.

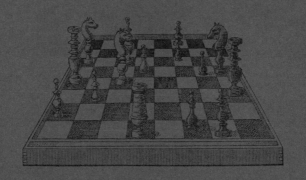

"You can discover more about a person in an hour of play than in a year of conversation."

PLATO

"The only wealth which you will keep forever is the wealth you have given away."

MARCUS AURELIUS

FREEDOM & ECONOMICS

The words "freedom" and "free" are perhaps the most overused and misrepresented words in the economic lexicon. Our current form of capitalism is proudly called "free market" capitalism, synonymous with political and individual freedom and the American way of life. We even export freedom to other nations, in the name of spreading democracy and therefore, free markets.

On closer inspection, this notion of "free" is not really free at all. In fact, the current "free market" economy is predicated on a number of rules and regulations, designed for a certain narrow kind of freedom, namely the freedom to profit from whatever the hell we like, regardless of the human or environmental costs.

Interestingly, the United States, whilst strongly advocating free markets and the freedom of the individual, locks away more people than anywhere else in the world. The U.S. houses a quarter of the world's prisoners, which means that, as of 2011, approximately 2.3 million people were behind bars. For some, this disturbingly high number of prisoners is great news. A very small group of private companies are making huge profits from imprisoning young men and women, often for non-violent, drug-related offences that could be treated more effectively through education and rehabilitation. Political comedian Bill Maher is quoted as saying:

> Prisons used to be a non-profit business... The CCA and similar corporations actually lobby Congress for stiffer sentencing laws so they can lock more people up and make more money. That's why America has the world's largest prison population because actually rehabilitating people would have a negative impact on the bottom line.

It's clear that the bottom line has sunk morally lower than at any other time in recent history. To raise the bottom line, we need new ways to reimagine, reinvent and redefine the language and principles that govern our current economic system. We need to create new ways to measure what is "valuable" in ourselves and in society. We need to create businesses that profit when people profit too, including our prisoners.

PEACE & ECONOMICS

Much has been said about the cost of war in recent years, but little has been imagined for the economic potential of peace. If we can spend $3.7 trillion pursuing an activity that results in death, destruction and bad-will, imagine if we spent the same amount on improving life, revamping education and creating lasting good-will.

Instead of the old economy that seeks profit from war and destruction, let's be part of the new economy of The Peace Industrial Complex. For this innovative and exciting industry, we call on a gung-ho private sector to put its entrepreneurial skills to work. There's profit in peace.

Here's one way to invest $3.7 trillion dollars (approx. $2 billion dollars a week) in the lucrative and growing peace sector:

We form a powerful company and call it, say, Happiburton Inc.

PHASE 1: OPERATION PEACE BOMB

Happiburton Inc. sends in 30,000 ground troops to conflict areas, consisting of designers, architects, engineers, nurses, teachers and graffiti artists to build hospitals, schools, playgrounds and cupcake parlors. These peace troops spread health, education and goodwill. Plus, nobody gets killed.

PHASE 2: CREATIVE SHOCK & AWE

We still have a few billion dollars left in the kitty so we build a free university, which quickly pays for itself because the faculty of Alternative Energy invents and patents revolutionary new alternative energies, generating billions of dollars of revenue for that country, continuing its free education and health care, which suddenly makes them less reliant on trading oil, less prone to corruption and less open to invasion from certain western democracies.

GROSS NATIONAL HAPPINESS

LIFE & ECONOMICS

How much is a life worth? Is it better to die with a million dollars in the bank or to have enjoyed life in a million different ways? Is a life better with more happiness or more money?

The question of how we value life is central to economics. What we value is what we end up working for. For most of us, life is a daily struggle between balancing our material goals with the pursuit of nonmaterial goals like love, leisure time, family, health, spirituality and community.

In today's market-based society, our lives are measured by our productivity, our bank balances and how much we consume. Social media companies value us for our personal data, which they mercilessly sell to advertisers for maximum profit.

We all feel the daily push and pull of "the market" on our souls, and it's hard to escape the invisible "profit at all costs" narrative that surrounds us. So, do we wait for governments and corporations to humanize the economy and prioritize our well-being, health and happiness? Or do we humanize the economy by changing the way we think, live, create and shop?

It's time for all lives to be valued and measured according to the joy, growth and harmony we bring to the planet, and each other. It's time we invested in kindness, community and love and divested from divisiveness, hatred and greed. Perhaps the world is ready for a new kind of bank, one that values and grows all the things that make life rich: *The Bank of Life Dollars.*

*"Nowadays people know
the price of everything
and the value of nothing."*

OSCAR WILDE

8

MEASURES OF SUCCESS

RE-IMAGINING THE STOCK MARKET

We've all seen the digitized screens of the New York Stock Exchange—
a set of scrolling numbers that symbolize the daily ups and downs of the
capitalist system. Behind these seemingly rational numbers are a whole world
of human emotions and desires, oscillating between fear and greed, hope and
envy. A rapid fluctuation of stock prices can either make grown men cry or
leap with euphoria. Such is the emotional power of the stock market.

By viewing the stock market as a collective expression of human desire,
we are able to curb the more negative forces that perpetuate the boom-
and-bust cycle. Conversely, by recalibrating the incentives of the market
to reward wiser, long-term thinking, our economic system will be more
profitable to more people over a longer period of time.

THE TRUE COST OF THINGS

Creativity is most powerful when we use it to shift the way we think about and experience everyday things. For example, if every time we purchased something we looked at the true cost of owning that thing, factoring in all the environmental and human costs involved in making and delivering that product to us, we would most likely buy more of the things that improve the world and less of the things that damage it. This shift in thinking would have a huge impact on the economy, simply by using our own consumer behavior to reshape economic patterns, forcing economists and brands to adopt more comprehensive and long-term thinking.

A TRUE LABEL

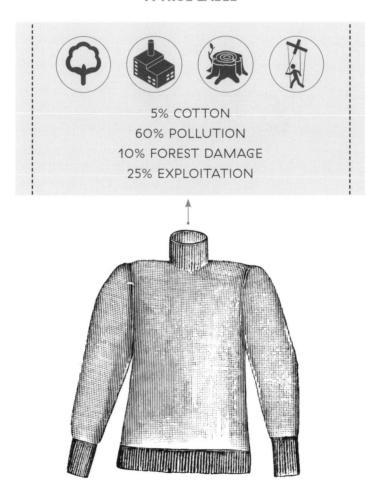

5% COTTON
60% POLLUTION
10% FOREST DAMAGE
25% EXPLOITATION

NOT ALL GROWTH IS GOOD

Pursuing the right kind of growth

"If we measure the wrong things, we'll do the wrong things."

JOSEPH STIGLITZ
Nobel Prize-winning Economist

The idea of growth for growth's sake is not only one-dimensional thinking, it is unsustainable, short-term economics. Like the American car industry that kept making gas-guzzling cars until it went broke, or the professional body-builder who kept taking steroids until his you-know-what shrunk to a pea, an economy that keeps measuring success by growth is bound to lose its mojo.

LIFE IS LONG IF YOU KNOW HOW TO LIVE IT.

"It is not that we have a short time to live,
but that we waste a lot of it.
Life is long enough, and a sufficiently generous
amount has been given to us for the highest
achievements if it were all well invested.
But when it is wasted in heedless luxury
and spent on no good activity, we are forced at last
by death's final constraint to realize that
it has passed away before we knew it was passing.
So it is: we are not given a short life but
we make it short, and we are not
ill-supplied but wasteful of it. . .
Life is long if you know how to use it."

SENECA THE YOUNGER

Roman Stoic philosopher & statesman
(c. 4 BC–AD 65)

THE NEW MEASURES

THE GENEROSITY INDEX

Generosity is a good indicator that people are happy and in a healthy financial state. When people help others for no specific reason, when they tip more, donate more to charity, we reckon the economy must be doing something right.

THE PROZAC INDICATOR

When people work harder to get a better life but, in the process, become less happy, the use of Prozac (or booze or other "happy drugs") increases. When the Prozac Index is up, we know the economy is down. It's time for an injection of Life Dollars.

THE OVER-PRICED ART INDICATOR

When banks are paying ridiculously large bonuses to their CEOs, bankers start buying ridiculously expensive art. When the value of art in our society is determined by banker bonuses, you know something is out of kilter and the bubble is about to burst. Time to sell your Warhols and Hirsts.

THE INTERNATIONAL SMILE INDEX

Possibly the simplest and most accurate measure of a thriving society and economy, the International Smile Index does not lie. Americans might rank highly on per capita income and GDP, but they rank sadly low on the International Smile Index.

GROSS NATIONAL HAPPINESS (GNH)

The term "Gross National Happiness" was coined by The King of Bhutan in 1972. He used the phrase to signal his commitment to building an economy that would serve Bhutan's unique culture based on Buddhist spiritual values, oriented around the belief that the beneficial development of human society can only take place when material and spiritual development complement and reinforce each other. The four pillars of GNH are the promotion of sustainable development; preservation and promotion of cultural values; conservation of the natural environment; and establishment of good governance. These four pillars transcend all cultures and are universal in their social and economic outcomes, regardless of culture or size of the nation.

It might be a small, relatively unknown nation, but Bhutan is not afraid to lead with big ideas. Here's a speech by Bhutan's Prime Minister, Jigmi Thinley, delivered to the United Nations in 2012:

> We need to rethink our entire growth-based economy so that we can thrive more effectively on our own resources in harmony with nature. We do not need to accept as inevitable a world of impending climate chaos and financial collapse. Economic growth is mistakenly seen as synonymous with well-being. The faster we cut down forests and haul in fish stocks to extinction, the more GDP (Gross Domestic Product) grows. Even crime, war, sickness and natural disasters make GDP grow, simply because these ills cause money to be spent. The global economic system is in rapid meltdown. It is based on the premise of limitless growth on a finite planet. It has produced ever-widening inequalities with 20% of the world now consuming 86% of its goods, while the poorest 20% consume 1% or less and emit 2% of the world's greenhouse gases. The world is in need of an international consensus for the creation of a new economic paradigm with well-being indicators, new national accounting systems that count natural and social capital and incentives for sustainable production. Our measures of progress and GNH index clearly show that producing and consuming more stuff does not make people happier. On the contrary, when they overwork and go into debt to buy ever more goods and pay the bills, they get more stressed. Working, producing and consuming less is not only good for nature but gives us more time to enjoy each other.

THE ECONOMIC KARMA LOOP OF
BEAUTIFUL ECONOMICS

A SUSTAINABLE IDEA

The elusive million-dollar business idea is out there. The great thing is, you don't need a million dollars to have a good idea. All you need is imagination and some brain-sweat. (Though fair-trade coffee and nicely fitting underwear will help.) Of course, not all ideas are good ideas, so it takes a smart investor to spot a gem.

CAPITAL

A smart and visionary investor-type gets behind the idea with business acumen and a wad of cash. The old investment principle of buy low/sell high applies here. The initial outlay (and risk) is relatively small compared to the huge upside of a great game-changing idea.

3-D PROFITS

Now something better exists in the world, whether it's a more efficient service, a healthier food product or a life-saving piece of technology.

INVESTMENT OPPORTUNITIES

Investing in creativity and creative people is akin to investing in stocks and bonds. In many cases, it's more rewarding.

THE BUSINESS CYCLE CONTINUES

Creativity is a resource that is never depleted. In fact, the more creative people and ideas you support or nourish, the more a business can grow and thrive.

DESIGN

To stay competitive in the marketplace, the product or service will need even more creative thinking to keep improving the product, as well as make it affordable to more people.

GROWTH

Suddenly, the creative idea needs people of all talents and skills to keep it alive: accountants, bookkeepers, engineers, electricians, painters, builders and workers of all shapes and sizes.

MALUS communis.   POMMIER commun. 117

a pinx.   Jarry sculp.

"You can get all As and still flunk life."

WALTER PERCY

LONG-TERM V. SHORT-TERM

The current economic "trash it now, pay later" model has little regard for its impact on future generations of fellow humans. Everything is based on short-term profits and the passing of responsibility onto someone else.

"I never attempt
to make money
on the stock market.
I buy on the assumption
that they could
close the market
the next day
and not reopen it
for five years."

WARREN BUFFETT

WANTED

Beautiful Economics Classifieds
The Smartest Girl in the Room

BEAUTIFUL ECONOMICS CLASSIFIEDS

DESPERATELY WANTED: Preschool Teacher

Must be able to make a mess, tell stories and face paint.
Fluent in Dr. Seuss an advantage. Proficiency with crayons a must.
Basic Salary $500,000 Life Dollars package + Scooter + 3 months
vacation a year.

NERVOUS ENERGY SCIENTIST

Seeking graduate in neuroscience or physics to join a start-up
business that converts the nervous energy of 8 million New Yorkers
into clean electrical energy to power school buses in underserved
communities, via the patented Human Nervous Energy Converter
App. Salary $100,000 + $500,000 Life Dollars + Bonus.

CEO PEACE INDUSTRIAL COMPLEX

PEACE!
A goldmine of opportunity!
We are seeking individuals interested in the new economy, The
Peace Economy. Must be prepared to make a killing saving lives.
Motivated by both morals and money. Must be an ambitious big
thinker. Huge Goldman Sachs-like bonuses based on number of
lives saved. Business travel to the world's most exciting peace-in-
process zones.
TASK:
To build relations and develop Weapons of Mass Education,
empathy & understanding.
Salary $280,000 + Life Dollars
+ Profit Share + Bonus
+ Potential Nobel Prize
+ Hang out with Bono

NURSE

Masters in human compassion. Soldier-like ability to face life and death on a daily basis. Possess the complex psychological skill of making sick patients smile. Manage and counsel stressed-out, overworked doctors. Put up with grumpy patients. Unflappable Strength of Character required. Starting salary $300,000, plus bonus for every person you help cure, Life Dollars and extra holidays.

LIFE DOLLARS INVESTMENT ADVISOR

You will be in charge of increasing the value of ordinary people's lives, through trading in the international currency of Life Dollars. Your performance will be measured by:
— Amount of quality time your clients spend with family
— The increase in client's mental and physical wealth, decrease in anger and booms in overall happiness

JOBS
for
GENTLE WORLD DOMINATION

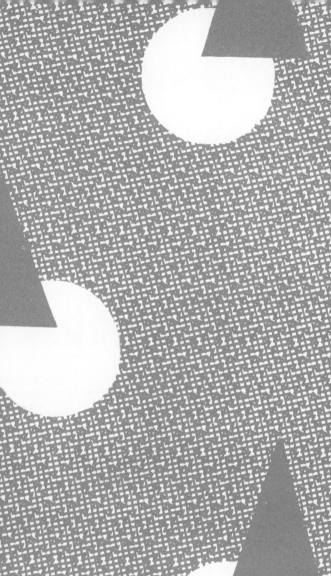

THE SMARTEST GIRL IN THE ROOM

Education and learning are subject to market forces in the same way crude oil or coffee prices are. Because of the inordinately high salaries offered to young graduates in tech and finance, these industries attract some of the best minds of our generation, diverting brilliant people from important occupations that pay less.

So, what if we turned the model around and incentivized our best and brightest to become schoolteachers or Alternative Energy engineers? Or designers of enlightened human experiences with a spiritual luxury brand. Wouldn't society and investors profit more in the long run?

But who will fund these investments? Investors in successful, modern companies like Apple, Google and Facebook will tell you there's plenty of money to be made in products or services that help human beings connect with each other deeply, inspire learning or experience a sense of childlike wonder or play.

All we need are visionary investors with big imaginations.

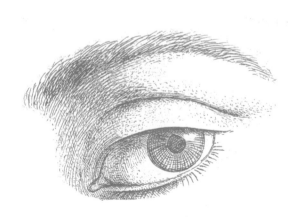

SUMMARY

The Triple Bottom Line

Storydoers

Acknowledgments

About

THE TRIPLE BOTTOM LINE
OF BEAUTIFUL ECONOMICS

The measure of a company's success is typically judged by the "bottom line," the declaration of financial profit or loss in a given period. All other considerations, like human or environmental costs, are irrelevant in this singular and narrow worldview.

But a new breed of company is redefining success by pursuing a Triple Bottom Line: a set of objectives that seek to increase the growth of people, planet and profit. Companies like Kickstarter, Warby Parker and Patagonia are not only achieving the Triple Bottom Line, they are thriving because of it.

This is further proof that people are putting their money where their values are, and are willing to develop long-term relationships with brands that stand for doing good, while doing good business.

STORYDOERS

There is no such thing as "creative types" and "economist types," but there are curious and highly motivated types. We all have the ability to imagine, think sideways and take calculated leaps of faith—we just have to be disciplined enough to play more, bold enough to imagine more, hardworking enough to turn the story into action.

Don't be afraid to fail and be open to criticism. Step out of your comfort zone and cross-pollinate with the most unlikely people of all backgrounds, cultures and professions. We need musicians working together with venture capitalists, architects collaborating with farmers, yoga teachers brainstorming with military generals and artists mapping out the future with economists. When we share knowledge and visions across different disciplines and mindsets, truly visionary ideas emerge.

So, whatever your background or creative talent, you can now be part of, and influence, a new economic movement. Wherever you encounter the evidence of Ugly Economics, view it as an opportunity to put your untapped creativity to work, whether by campaigning, or inventing a better product, service or way of living. A new economics starts with a new narrative, and you are a key protagonist in the story.

"Every man must decide whether he will walk in the light of creative altruism or the darkness of destructive selfishness…"

MARTIN LUTHER KING, JR.

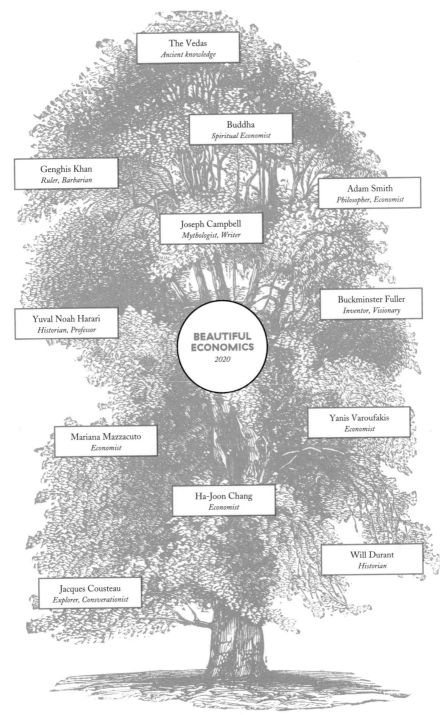

The Vedas
Ancient knowledge

Buddha
Spiritual Economist

Genghis Khan
Ruler, Barbarian

Adam Smith
Philosopher, Economist

Joseph Campbell
Mythologist, Writer

Buckminster Fuller
Inventor, Visionary

Yuval Noah Harari
Historian, Professor

BEAUTIFUL
ECONOMICS
2020

Yanis Varoufakis
Economist

Mariana Mazzacuto
Economist

Ha-Joon Chang
Economist

Will Durant
Historian

Jacques Cousteau
Explorer, Consverationist

Some key figures and ideas that helped grow this book.
Special thanks to Francesca Richer and powerHouse Books, and to John Foster for early creative input.

Creativity is the most precious
natural resource.

ABOUT

Howard Collinge never studied economics at Harvard Business School and he will definitely not be invited to speak at Davos. He is not even an Influencer. He is however, Founder and CEO of The Bank of Life Dollars; has worked as a Creative Director on four continents with the world's most successful brands, and has taught Strategic Design at The New School. He currently lives in New York with his wife and eight-week-old daughter and works with institutions that believe in the power of a meaningful, well-told story.

CREDITS

dress suit from the late Victorian, early Edwardian period. Image provided by iStock.com, used with permission. Page 64: *Cabbage Rose (Rosa Centifolia)* from *Traité des Arbres et Arbustes que l'on Cultive en France en Pleine Terre* (1801–1819) by Pierre-Joseph Redouté. Original from the New York Public Library. Image provided by rawpixel, used with permission. Page 66: *Popular Lectures on Human Nature*, a book cover illustration by an unknown artist referencing Prof. W.G. Alexander. Original from Library of Congress. Image provided by rawpixel, used with permission. Page 70: Vintage Victorian style blooming flowers engraving. Original from the British Library. Image provided by rawpixel, used with permission. Page 71: "Mahatma Gandhi with a mustache." Photo by Ari Manoharan. Used with permission under a creative commons license. Page 72: Andy Warhol. (Public domain). Page 73: Factory from *Pittsburgh's Progress, Industries and Resources* (1886) published by George H. Thurston. Original from the British Library. Image provided by rawpixel, used with permission. Page 76: Egg timer from *Philozoia: Or Moral Reflections on the Actual Condition of the Animal Kingdom, and on the Means of Improving the Same* (1839) by Thomas Forster. Original from the British Library. Image provided by rawpixel, used with permission. Page 79: Teacup engraving. (Public domain). Page 84: *Dish from A Paper Lantern for Puseyites* (1843) published by Georgiana Zornlin. Original from the British Library. Image provided by rawpixel, used with permission. Page 87: Vintage Victorian style horseshoe engraving. Original from the British Library. Image provided by rawpixel, used with permission. Page 88: *Autumn and Water* illustration by Bijutsu Sekai (1893–1896) by Watanabe Seitei, a prominent Kacho-ga artist. Image provided by rawpixel, used with permission. Page 89: Crowned crane from *Adventures in the far interior of South Africa;*

including a journey to Lake Ngami, nd rambles in Honduras. To which is appended a short treatise on the best mode of skinning and preserving Birds, Animals* (1866) published by J Leyland. Original from the British Library. Image provided by rawpixel, used with permission. Page 90: 'Surf-Swimming'—or surfing—in Polynesia in the 19th century. Illustration from *"Royal Geographical Readers no. 5" of Asia, Africa, America and Oceania*, publ. T Nelson & Sons, London in 1883. Image provided by iStock.com, used with permission. Page 93: Dalai Lama Tenzin Gyatso (Public domain). Page 96: *Unicorn*, 1806, by Friedrich Johann Justin Bertuch (1747–1822). (Public domain). Page 98: "Oscar Wilde by Napoleon Sarony, 1882," photographic print on card mount. Library of Congress. Used with permission under a creative commons license. Page 99: Vintage European style key engraving from *Six Semaines de Vacances* by Paul Poiré (1880). Original from the British Library. Image provided by rawpixel, used with permission. Page 101: Chessboard, antique French engraving. Image provided by iStock.com, used with permission. Page 102: Marble portrait of the Emperor Marcus Aurelius, Anonymous (Roman Empire). Collection: Walters Art Museum. Used with permission under a creative commons license. Page 105: Flower engraving. (Public domain). Page 106: Fleur de lys of the board room from *Artistic And Historical Guide At The Palais De Fontainebleau, Etc.* (1889). Original from the British Library. Image provided by rawpixel, used with permission. Page 107: Quarter. (Public domain). Page 110: Banner. (Public domain). Page 111: Top: icon art from Noun Project, by, from left: Margarita Escoto, parkjisun, Ben Hantoot, Juan Pablo Bravo. Bottom: illustration from "Lindeman Catalogue," (1895). Image provided by iStock.com, used with permission. Page 112: Illustration from "Catalogue of Different Goods,"

(1895). Image provided by iStock.com, used with permission. Page 114: Celestial double crescent moon with stars line art design element. Image provided by rawpixel, used with permission. Page 115: Dragon. (Public domain). Page 117: Apple, Malus Communis from *Traité des Arbres et Arbustes que l'on Cultive en France en Pleine Terre* (1801–1819) by Pierre-Joseph Redouté. Original from the New York Public Library. Image provided by rawpixel, used with permission. Page 123: Canvas from *Zes Putti Tonen een Doek Met Tekst* (1759) by Cornelis Ploos van Amstel. Original from The Rijksmuseum. Image provided by rawpixel, used with permission. Page 124: "Endleaves of Art. Taste. Beauty" (1931) by anonymous. Original from The Rijksmuseum. Image provided by rawpixel, used with permission. Page 125: Detail, *Studies of Eyes* (1630–1640) by Jusepe de Ribera. Original from The Rijksmuseum. Image provided by rawpixel, used with permission. Page 128: Ice cream in a waffle cone, with cherry, by Evgeniy Zotov. Image provided by iStock.com, used with permission. Page 129: Steel engraving of engineer Otto Lilienthal after photography of Ottomar Anschütz. Original from "Gartenlaube" (1894). Image provided by iStock.com, used with permission. Page 130: Candle light from *Philozoia: Or Moral Reflections on the Actual Condition of the Animal Kingdom, and on the Means of Improving the Same* by Thomas Forster (1839). Original from the British Library. Image provided by rawpixel, used with permission. Page 131: Common Lime tree, *Tilia europaea*, U.K., 1880–1889. Image provided by iStock.com, used with permission. Page 133: Victorian style typewriter engraving. Original from the British Library. Image provided by rawpixel, used with permission. Back cover: Vintage Victorian style atlas engraving. Original from the British Library. Image provided by rawpixel, used with permission.

Beautiful Economics:
A Guide to Gentle World Domination
Text and images © 2015, 2021 Howard Collinge

Published in the United States by powerHouse Books,
a division of powerHouse Cultural Entertainment, Inc.
32 Adams Street, Brooklyn, NY 11201-1021
e-mail: info@powerHouseBooks.com
website: www.powerHouseBooks.com

www.beautifuleconomics.com

Second edition, 2021

Library of Congress Control Number: 2020949503

ISBN 978-1-57687-969-6

Designed by Francesca Richer
Printed by Toppan Leefung

10 9 8 7 6 5 4 3 2 1

Printed and bound in China